D0113658

I Wish I Knew It

BEFORE GOING *to* COLLEGE

Gabbriel SIMONE

New York

GAIL BORDEN
PUBLIC LIBRARY DISTRICT
ELGIN, ILLINOIS

I Wish I Knew It
BEFORE GOING *to* COLLEGE

by Gabbriel Simone

© 2012 Gabbriel Simone. All rights reserved.

No part of this publication may be reproduced or transmitted in any form or by any means, mechanical or electronic, including photocopying and recording, or by any information storage and retrieval system, without permission in writing from author or publisher (except by a reviewer, who may quote brief passages and/or show brief video clips in a review).

Disclaimer: The Publisher and the Author make no representations or warranties with respect to the accuracy or completeness of the contents of this work and specifically disclaim all warranties, including without limitation warranties of fitness for a particular purpose. No warranty may be created or extended by sales or promotional materials. The advice and strategies contained herein may not be suitable for every situation. This work is sold with the understanding that the Publisher is not engaged in rendering legal, accounting, or other professional services. If professional assistance is required, the services of a competent professional person should be sought. Neither the Publisher nor the Author shall be liable for damages arising herefrom. The fact that an organization or website is referred to in this work as a citation and/or a potential source of further information does not mean that the Author or the Publisher endorses the information the organization or website may provide or recommendations it may make. Further, readers should be aware that internet websites listed in this work may have changed or disappeared between when this work was written and when it is read.

ISBN 978-1-61448-087-7 paperback
ISBN 978-1-61448-088-4 eBook
Library of Congress Control Number: 2011933996

Published by:
MORGAN JAMES PUBLISHING
The Entrepreneurial Publisher
5 Penn Plaza, 23rd Floor
New York City, New York 10001
(212) 655-5470 Office
(516) 908-4496 Fax
www.MorganJamesPublishing.com

Cover Design by:
Rachel Lopez
rachel@r2cdesign.com

Interior Design by:
Bonnie Bushman
bbushman@bresnan.net

In an effort to support local communities, raise awareness and funds, Morgan James Publishing donates one percent of all book sales for the life of each book to Habitat for Humanity.
Get involved today, visit
www.HelpHabitatForHumanity.org.

To My Brother

CONTENTS

INTRODUCTION

What do you think college is like? Class, sex and parties? Some of your ideas may be accurate but I will assure you that much of what you think is actually inaccurate. There is so much about college that you don't know. I'm referring to the preconceived ideas that high school students might predict. Maybe your brother or sister is in college now and, lucky for you, you have more insight into college life than many high school students. I've put this book together so that you can discover the ins, the outs, the ups and the downs of a college experience. There are so many opportunities that students are not aware of that are available at colleges and universities around the country and the world. You have four, or for some of you five or six years to make something of yourself and your future. You will arrive at college looking towards what you will become but you will also find out who you are. College is the best and fastest four years of your life. Has anybody told you how to make the most of them?

Consider the many aspects of college you will need to balance: school work, clubs, sporting events, personal health, social life, roommates, girlfriends, boyfriends, professors, friends, family, work, and yes, classes, sex, and parties; this list is nearly never ending. You may be confident that you can already balance all of those aspects at home. Who cares? That's home. Home, with friends, family and strong support systems close by. This is college.

Are you making yourself ready for college? Do you really know what to expect? College is a significant step and change in a person's life. Once it begins it is a fresh start. There is opportunity for success but there is also opportunity available for failure which is unfortunately easier to achieve than most realize.

Your college experience will solely rely on what you make of it, what you put in is what you will get back. Choosing and learning what you will put into it is the key. Here, at college, no one will be by your side telling you to get involved, do extracurricular activities, or go to sporting events supporting your school. You will need to be proactive and get involved because you want to.

If you want to succeed, you can and will. If you don't care, you will struggle. There are unlimited opportunities and it is up to you to explore them. It is about finding yourself, who you really are.

Now you ask, how do I do this? You can learn by just doing. You can learn from your mistakes. Or you can learn from those who have been there and that is exactly what you are about to read. The following stories come from college students who responded to the saying, "I wish I knew it, before going to college." Use their stories, use their advice. This is your heads up on the ups, downs, ins, outs, the good, the bad, and the ugly.

This is something I wish I had when I was going into college. It is a common sense, easy read book. There are no hidden messages.

There is nothing to analyze. Working in college admissions I saw firsthand how much high school students didn't know what they were really getting themselves into. Many of them, as I said before, thought college is going to class and partying. While that is not entirely true, class and parties are part of college. In fact, here are some stories you will read in this book, "I wish I knew how easy it was for relationships to get out of hand at college," "I wish I knew that the supply of alcohol doesn't run out at college," and "I wish

I knew that the walk of shame really happens." That's the fun stuff right? Relationships, drinking and hooking up. Now what about these... "I wish I knew how much I would appreciate my parents," "I wish I knew people could make reputations for themselves in one weekend," and "I wish I knew the value of silence before I came to college." There are so many great points and common sense thoughts throughout this book to keep you entertained but also teach you a thing or two or maybe one hundred new things to be aware of as you venture into this new chapter of your life. Enjoy!

PART I

THE TRANSITION

FAMILY

FRIENDS

FINDING YOU

I wish I knew that college wasn't about becoming somebody new but rather it's about finding who you really are. When I was getting ready to leave for college I thought about all the things I wanted to do. I wanted to always care about how I looked. I wanted to bring cool purses and change them when I wore different outfits. I wanted to be in charge of all the big student events on campus because I thought event planners were so cool. I thought so much about how I wanted to be like certain people. I tried so hard to do things that I thought were cool. Unfortunately I didn't like anything I was doing. How was this possible? How was I so unhappy?

When I took some time to think about it I realized I was doing things to become something new and something that I thought I liked. I never took the time to think about who I really was. Why am I working so hard to be like other people? Those people are already who they are. I should just be me.

I started to pay more attention to how I felt towards certain things. Little by little I picked up on what I enjoyed. By adding more to my plate I had a much better idea of what I liked. I had a much better idea of what my abilities were. I had a much better idea of what I could accomplish. Some of the most successful people in life are successful because they love what they do. I made it my goal to find what I loved. I knew that if I could find my passion, I could make it my life. I would make it my career and I would be happy. I am glad that I finally know who I am. I wish somebody told me sooner to just be me.

I wish I knew not to trust anyone too quickly. First impressions aren't always what they seem.

BE WHO YOU WANT TO BE

I wish I knew that you could be whoever you wanted to be and do whatever you wanted to do. Nobody has any prejudgments about you. If you want to join a club, a sorority, fraternity, run for student government, or anything else you can do it. Nobody can say that that isn't you because nobody knows you or what you like. Just because you were known for one thing in high school doesn't mean you have to stick to that. If you are comfortable with who you were than continue to be that person but if you want to try something new and make a name for yourself as something different then go for it. **There are endless possibilities; you can explore yourself to your fullest potential**. Think about who you want to be before you arrive.

MY PARENTS "BABIED" ME

I wish I knew just how hard the transition would be leaving my parents. I had a family where everything was given to me and everything was very accessible. When I came to school it seemed as though this all changed. I had to make my own food, get up in the morning and do my own laundry. I knew all of this was going to happen but it's a lot harder to adjust to than people realize. It actually made me depressed because it made me think about how much my family did for me and supported me. I felt kind of alone.

On top of that school was also much harder. My teachers and my parents babied me throughout high school. In high school I had everything laid out for me. It didn't at all prepare me for the college lifestyle. Now, if I have an issue with one of my classes I can't go to my Mom to fix it, I have to resolve it myself. Easier said than done.

KNOWING MY SELF MORE

I wish I knew more about myself. Then again, that is the point of college-to learn about yourself, your strengths and weaknesses, your personal limits, your priorities, and your goals. When you're in college, take the time to learn about yourself. Take risks – meet with professors, e-mail employers, study abroad, try new things, meet new people, and have fun but don't go out of control. Keep an eye on your schoolwork, get good grades and take advantage of academic opportunities on campus to learn about careers. Don't let anyone hold you back. Did I mention meet new people? Go outside your comfort zone and you will be pleasantly surprised. Before you know it, you will become the person you always wanted to be.

WE ARE ALL DIFFERENT PEOPLE

I wish I knew how different people across the U.S. were. I am a foreigner to the southern culture of the U.S. I grew up in a very small town in the Northeast and what I was used to was completely different than the crowed town I was now in, in the south. My school opened my eyes in a sense for a whole new world; a whole new lifestyle. I knew that people in the South were going to be culturally different than the people from my home town but I wish I prepared for those differences.

I focused so much on pointing out people's differences that I was limiting myself to friendships and to enjoying what my school had to offer. As different as I was to a lot of the people from the south I was in the same situation that they were in. They were different to me and I was different to them.

NO REMINDERS OF THE PAST

I wish I knew that the past starts to fade. No matter what you were like in high school, none of that affects the person you are seen as by the thousands of new people you meet at college. That being said, college gives you the chance to evaluate the things from the past that you may not like about yourself and eliminate them for your "new" personality that you are ready to present to your new college friends.

Before I came to college, I dealt with my father having cancer. **Throughout high school I was known as the kid with the sick Dad.** I found that once I got to college I was happy that I didn't have to think about the past as much. Nobody was asking how my Dad was. Nobody was sympathizing with me when I was having a bad day and teachers weren't treating me like a baby. I wasn't constantly being reminded that my Dad was once sick. I finally was viewed as just me and no longer the boy with the sick Dad.

I wish I knew not to burn any bridges with the people I met. You never know when you might have to work with them or when you may need them to help you with something.

SHOULD HAVE TRAVELED

I wish I knew how difficult it was going to be going to college when I had never traveled alone in high school. My freshman year I was extremely homesick and I had a really hard time dealing with problems on my own. I was always used to working out problems with my mom or my close friends. Even though there were girls all around me at college, none of them were my friends yet. **I never had to deal with anything on my own before college**.

When I was in high school I never traveled without my family. I think if I had traveled more, with friends or even a weekend school trip I would have been more prepared for the transition to college. If I had traveled on my own at one time I may have gotten a taste of what it would have been like to be alone. I would have gotten a taste of what it would have been like to lay in bed and talk to my mom on the phone rather than sit with her in person. I wish I would have traveled before college so I would have known a little more about independence.

FREEDOM

I wish I knew how much freedom I would actually have. I was the baby of my family. My brother was 10 years older and my sister was 8 years older. Because of that I was never able to make my own mistakes. My brother and sister made the mistakes for me. As a result of that I was often not allowed to do much besides play my sport and go to school. I was definitely not allowed to go to parties unless I snuck out of the house. Then I went to college. There are no rules set by your parents and you are free to do whatever you want whenever you want. I have homework tonight but will I do it? Nope, I would rather drink or hang out with my friends. This was my major downfall first semester. **I would always put fun over work.** This hurt my grades my freshman year and it is all catching up to me now. I wish I would have known about freedom before I came to school.

Keeping your head on straight and realizing that you are actually at college is one of the most important things. Do not let the freedom bring you down; it is probably the hardest thing to manage while away at school.

APPRECIATING MY UPBRINGING

I wish I knew to appreciate the way my parents raised me. My family raised me to respect others. They raised me to clean up after myself. At college I began to appreciate the times my Mom yelled at me to clear my plate, to put away the dishes, to vacuum my room, and to keep my house neat. It was clear to see that other people are not considerate of your surroundings. Some of my friends were clearly babied their whole life. Their parents probably cleaned the house, set and cleared the table and took care of any problems around the house. I could tell because so many of my friends are complete slobs. They expected others, including myself to clean up after them.

I used to clean up after them all the time because I liked my apartment to be clean. It always made me mad that they were such slobs but the thing is I'm not their parents. Because of that I started to just keep my room the way I liked it and didn't let their mess bother me. After a while they realized how disgusting they were and they began to clean up after themselves. I wish I knew to appreciate the times my parents were hard on me. It has made me a much better person that a lot of the people I have met at college.

I wish I knew I wasn't saying "goodbye" to my friends from home, I was actually saying "see you later."

IF YOU WANT IT...
GO GET IT

I wish I knew that nothing would be handed to me. I think I always knew that nothing in life would be handed to me but I never knew the benefits of actually getting off my butt and going to get what I wanted. To get into college I had to do well in high school, I had to apply to college, go for admissions interviews and so on. Nobody handed me a place at college.

Now, just because I got into college it didn't mean that I would be handed a job at the end of four years. **As long as I did well in my classes and didn't get into trouble I would be handed a diploma and a hand shake.** No job was going to be handed and in fact no good grades would be handed to me. The reason that I wish I knew this sooner was because it wasn't until my junior year that I realize my actions had an effect on the outcome. I went to all of my classes and studied for my exams. I then got good grades. Funny how that works right? I went to career fairs and met with my career counselor. She helped clean up my resume and I got a great internship. This all sounds like common sense but when you are surrounded and influenced by college students who are for the most part lazy, it takes some self motivation to get a step ahead.

Everything that I have accomplished thus far I have gone out and got myself. I've gone through the rest of college expecting that nobody will hand me anything and the results I've been getting are better than I expected. It shows others that I'm a hard worker and it proves to me that hard work does pay off.

MY DAD

I wish I knew that my Dad was someone I could talk to about my feelings. When I got to school I found myself alone among friends, lacking the trust in other people to talk about my inner thoughts or problems I was facing. **I started talking to my Dad more** about things I was noticing at school. It was like he was a pillow for me to lie on. Our weekly conversations became phone calls that I looked forward to. We talked about everything from girls, to class, partying and yes, how much I missed my Mom. Our relationship grew with every phone call. I wish

I knew this before college because I now feel like I missed out on forming a great relationship with my Dad when I was actually living at home.

MISSING HOME

I wish I knew that it's okay to miss home because everyone does at some point. Not only did I miss my parents but I missed my dog, my bed, my room, and the comfort of sitting in my living room or at my kitchen table. But here's the thing, no matter how much you miss home try hard to cherish the time you have at college because it is truly the best 4 years of your life and it goes by so fast! If you make an effort to enjoy your school you will find yourself not wanting to go home as much. It does take time but once you are comfortable with your new environment you will be able to take advantage of the things your school has to offer.

MY PARENTS

I wish I knew how much I would appreciate my parents. I learned to appreciate them a lot more when I went to college. I noticed the sacrifices they made for me. I never reflected on what they have done for me when I was in high school. When I came to college I had a lot of free time, especially at night while laying in my bed, to think about my parents. I thought about all the times they woke up to drive me to practices early on the weekends.

As I listened to my friends talk about all of the school loans they were building up I thought about all the hours my Dad spent working to save up money so that he could pay for my college. As I walked down three flights of stairs to get to the laundry room I really began to appreciate the times my Mom washed my clothes. Worst of all as I sat in front of the microwave waiting for my macaroni and cheese to be done I appreciated the food my parents used to cook for me. Life was easy in high school and the biggest reason for that was because my parents were always there for me. I wish I knew how much I would appreciate them when I came to college because I would have said "Thank You" a lot more when I was in high school. Thanks Mom and Dad!

DIFFERENT

I wish I knew that everyone has a different story. Coming from an inner city area I met people who had completely different backgrounds than me. Most of my friends now are from towns in New York and New Jersey. Their lives were completely different than mine. They lived in neighborhoods and went to the beach on a regular basis. For the first time ever, I had to defend being a New England sports fan.

The best part of realizing that my new friends were so different was sharing our stories. We realized that we aren't as different as we thought. **Surprisingly, even coming from different backgrounds we had a lot of things in common.** All of us were huge sports fans and while we loved watching sports together the Boston, New York rivalry sometimes caused some tension. The hole in the wall of my room was a result of the Giants winning the Super Bowl. I swear it was justified.

IT ONLY TOOK TWO

I wish I knew that it only took two great friends to make college exciting. I expected to come to college and make hundreds of friends. It turns out that while I hung out with a large amount of people I really only had two great friends and that's all I needed. My "weekend" friends were great to party with and great to hang out with but I didn't trust that any of them would run to my side if I needed help or if I were getting in trouble. When you are far from home it is important to find one or two great friends. Large groups of friends will come and go and that's okay. If you can find a couple great friends I consider you lucky.

MAKING FRIENDS

I wish I knew that making friends wasn't going to be as hard as I thought. I used to be really nervous of that fact I would be living in a different sate with none of my friends from high school. "Would I fit in?" and "Would I get along with people?" were some of the questions that used to run through my head. These thoughts went through my head even more frequently the week before freshman year started.

Turns out it was all a waste of thinking. I lived in a suite freshman year and instantly became so close with my five other roommates. I became so close with each of them that we would find ourselves saying, **"It feels like we have known each other for so long."** My roommates at school ended up becoming like a family away from home for me. They were there when I needed them and made college fun and exciting. If I had known this before going away it would have made me much less nervous.

FREE TRIPS

I wish I knew I was going to have the best years of my life because I came to college. I had not known that being involved in student organizations would let me meet the best friends I would ever have. It helped me develop leadership skills that I still use to this day. A lot of the organizations at my school sponsor conferences and trips outside the state. I went on a free trip to New York City with my friends. The cost was completely paid for by the university because we were attending a conference. The best part about the trip was that I was going with my closest friends.

We all had a common interest, which brought us together within the club which then allowed us to travel to places like New York. Earlier that year we also got a free trip to California which was sponsored by the athletics department. They covered the cost of our trip because we were supporting the student athletes. **As long as you follow your passion**, college will introduce you to some of the best people you will ever meet and best experiences you will ever have.

FRIENDLY ADJUSTMENT

I wish I knew more about the adjustment of making friends. I had a very close group of friends in high school and since I had known them forever I never had to put a real effort into keeping those friends. I never had to worry about getting closer with them, it just happened naturally. I wish I knew that when making new friends at college, in order to keep them you really had to follow through to become closer. If you meet someone and you want to be friends with them, you have to make the effort yourself and not expect people to automatically be your friend. Don't assume they know everything about you the first time they meet you. Don't assume they will call you. I wish I knew this because then I would have definitely put more effort into making friends.

I would have also thought more about **how I wanted people to view me.** The way they looked at me was not how my high school friends viewed me. I should have thought about how I was going to approach meeting new people.

MAKE MORE FRIENDS

I wish I knew that you don't have to limit yourself to hanging out with the people in your dorm. Freshman year I only hung out with the guys on my floor. When I got sick of them I had nowhere to go to. If I wanted to be alone in my room I was still surrounded by my friends. I knew that I had to make an effort to find other friends to hang out with as well. I began to talk to more guys and girls from other dorms. I joined some organizations on campus to meet friends as well. It ended up benefiting me because I now had other friends to go hang out with other than the friends in my dorm. **I wish I knew how helpful these connections would be.** I should have branched out earlier in the year.

FRIENDLY PEOPLE... NOT

I wish I knew that people are friendly only when they want to make friends. When I came to college I expected everyone to be very friendly and social to each other because, except for a few limitations, no one really knows each other. Sometimes you may talk to someone online before school to make plans to hang out when you both get there. Well, don't plan on hanging out because that hardly ever happens.

I was happily surprised when I got to school last year and everyone was friendly to each other. This lasted all of 3 days. Then everyone seemed to suddenly agree to be finished with being nice to everyone. I am glad college lived up to what I believed it to be...for half a week.

OLD FRIEND, GOOD FRIENDS

I wish I knew how genuine my friends from home were. I took so much time trying to make friends at college that I slowly let my friends from high school slip away. When my school had a few days off for a holiday I was a little nervous to go back home. I didn't know how my friends would treat me. I felt guilty that I hadn't made an effort to keep in touch with all of them. When I finally went home and saw my old friends I got a feeling that I had missed so much. I felt comfort and familiarity.

My friends from home and I picked up our friendships as if no time had passed. It took no effort to make each other laugh. We had a history and no matter how much we didn't talk in college my friends from home were like family. I wish I knew not to worry so much about losing my friends from home. If I didn't talk to them for months we could still pick up from where we left off.

DON'T JUDGE A BOOK BY ITS COVER

I wish I knew not to judge somebody just by what you see online. I thought my roommate and I were not going to get along at all because his profile was completely different than any of my current friends. His interests were different than mine and he didn't look anything like the friends I hung out with. This was such a bad thing to do because I went into freshman year with a bad impression. It turns out he was nothing like what I had imagined. He still had different interests than I did but he introduced me to hobbies that I would have never imagined trying. When I was in high school I never exposed myself to different things beyond what I was used to. It was partially because my friends in high school shared all the same hobbies as me. We would just stick to what we were used to.

I am a senior now and my roommate and I have been living together for the past 4 years. He has become one of my best friends. I am lucky that we got along but I feel bad that I went into freshman year thinking the way I thought.

RIVAL HIGH SCHOOLS

I wish I knew I could be friends with kids from rival high schools. When I came to college I bumped into a few guys from a rival high school. I automatically didn't like them because of that. Worse than that, two of my roommates were from rival schools. It took me time to give them a chance and become friends with them. Eventually I came to realize it didn't matter anymore. We were now at the same school rooting for the same team. The guys ended up being really cool. Even when we went home for the breaks we hung out. Friends at home think it's weird but it has made the high school games more exciting. We still cheer for our own high school teams but when one of our teams win, usually mine, it makes bragging rights so much sweeter.

HOME SWEET HOME

I wish I knew the appreciation I would grow for my town, friends and family. **Starting from scratch is hard and at times all I wanted was to hug my dad or take a drive to one of the beaches in my town.** I missed the friends I had through high school but had to remind myself not to let it get in the way of making new friends. First impressions are the ones that last so I made sure to have a good attitude and always appear approachable to those around me.

I am not the type of person to instigate plans, but here, sometimes I had to be. I met a girl in my English class that seemed nice and we had the same major so I friend requested her. I asked if she wanted to meet up for lunch. We looked into a few clubs together and bonded over similar experiences and now are pretty good friends. It is important to put yourself out there and remember that everyone's in the same boat as you.

REPUTATIONS

I wish I knew that people could make reputations for themselves in one weekend. When I came to school I was looking forward to having a good time on the weekends but I was also hesitant to jump right into the party scene. The first weekend I decided I would get dressed up and go out with my friends but I wasn't going to drink. It was probably one of the best decisions I made.

Within one night of partying, girls and guys had quickly made reputations for themselves. You could pick out the heavy drinkers, the sluts, the party people, the stoners, and so on. It was crazy. To this day, now as a senior, I still think about those people the same as I do many other people. Reputations stick, you can make one for yourself in two minutes and it may take you three or four years to get rid of them, if you're lucky. Usually you never get rid of them. If you're looking to keep a good reputation I suggest you lay low on the heavy partying, at least in the beginning of your freshman year.

FRIENDSHIPS: COLLEGE VS. HIGH SCHOOL

I wish I knew what friendships were going to be like in college. The level of friendships you make in college is on a whole other level than the friendships in high school. Everyone still has their high school friends but for me the friendships I made in college were much stronger. In high school I had the same group of friends since middle school. We stuck together all through middle school and high school because it is not common to just leave your group of friends. I'm not saying that I was forced to have the friends I had but even if I felt that they weren't the right "fit" for me I still kept them as friends because we had a history together.

The friends I made in college I made because they are similar to me. We all had a common interest in the beginning, that's why we became friends in the first place. It wasn't because our parents were friends or we had known each other all of our lives. **I have no doubt that these people** will always be in my life and that our bonds will continue to get stronger.

I wish I knew to stay true to who I was and not let my friends form the person I am.

PART II

DORM ROOM

ROOMMATES

CLOTHES

BATHROOM

CLEAN ROOM CLEAN MIND

I wish I knew that the more stuff I brought to school the more stress I brought onto myself. Freshman year I brought way too much stuff from home to school. I don't have any older brothers or sisters so I had no idea what was really needed. I brought just about all of my clothes and used only about one third of them when I was at school. Along with the other stresses of school, I would come back to my room and my side of the room was always a mess. I had clothes hanging out of my drawers and I had so much clutter on my desk. **All I wanted when I came back to my room from class was a simple and clean room to clear my head.** Instead I came back from a stressful class to a stressful room.

Halfway through the year I brought home a ton of my stuff. I rearranged my room and kept only what I needed. The second half of the year felt so much easier. In the mornings when I had to get dressed I no longer stood in my room trying to decide what to wear. Everything that was in my closet I liked so picking out an outfit took seconds. Also, when I came back to my room after class I had plenty of clear desk space to get organized and do work on. I wish I knew that a clean and simple room would help reduce the other stresses at college.

I wish I knew not to stay up until 3:00am every morning.

SCARED

I wish knew that everyone is scared before going to college. It seems silly, but moving out to college from home into a room with other girls, a bed, a desk and a dresser was at first traumatizing to me. Of course I cried and was fearful of how others would behave. I was afraid that I would not be accepted by others. Then I would watch the other girls as they left the room unannounced to go to the bench outside to call their parents. Many times I saw my roommates or other girls in my hall crying at the bench while they were on the phone. More times than I expected, they would walk back from being on their phone with tears in their eyes. I always thought I was the only "baby" who cried because they missed home.

I always tried to hide that I was upset but as I saw other girls crying it made me feel better. In fact, it was one thing that brought me and my friends together. As strange as it sounds, one night we all talked about our parents, families and friends from home and cried together and it made us feel so much better. It actually brought us together more. I wish I knew that I wasn't the only one scared.

I wish I knew it was okay to bring your stuffed animals to college.

DIRTY DUDES

I wish I knew that not everyone is as clean as me. I am a clean dude; my parents raised me to clean up after myself. I thought it was a normal habit to clean up after yourself. Wrong! **The majority of my friends are dirty.** They never clean up after themselves. Imagine what a guy's bathroom would look like after not cleaning it for weeks. Now multiply that image but 100 and that's what our bathroom looked like. I wish I knew to prepare myself to deal with dirty people. I had to remind myself I'm not their parent and if they were nasty at this age there's not much hope. It took some time but I started to keep only my room clean and didn't let the other stuff bother me. Thankfully, little by little they all realized how disgusting they were and began to clean up more.

SILENCE

I wish I knew the value of silence before going to college. When I was at home doing work I was usually someplace quiet where I could get all of my work done with few distractions. In college, unless I was hibernating in the library, the silence was hard to find. I had to deal with roommates, other students, outside distractions and generally a lot of background noise. **Headphones became my best friend.** Invest in a good pair and learn to appreciate them. I even sometimes wore them and pretended I was listening to music just so I could block out the noise around me.

I wish I knew how good I would get at playing video games and ordering late night pizza.

SURPRISE INTERESTS

I wish I knew the importance of spending time with your roommates even if they seem to have different interests than you. I knew some friends from home that came to the same college. As soon as I moved in to my room I went right to my friend's room. I spent so much time with him that I never really got to know my roommates. One night my friend left for the weekend so I was kind of stuck with just my roommates. We ended up talking for the entire night. We had some things in common but surprisingly the new things I learned about him I found really interesting. For example he is an avid fan of the gym. I always regretted not going to the gym or working out when I was in high school. Part of the reason I didn't was because my friends didn't either. After talking with my roommate that night I decided I would go to the gym with him the next day. Since then I have gone to the gym just about every day. It is one of my new favorite hobbies and it makes me feel great.

I learned something new about myself after opening up to my roommate. I would have never gone to the gym had I not talked to him that night.

I realized I was limiting myself by hanging out with the same friends from high school. Did I like other things that I didn't know about? I decided to join some clubs at school to find out. We get e-mails every week telling us what organizations have meetings that week. I usually always delete them but one week I decided to read though them and go to a few meetings. I ended up joining a couple of clubs that week. I wish I knew to join them sooner. It was such a nice break from my immediate circle of friends. By meeting new people I found that I had interests in things that I would have never thought of. I sometimes feel like the most important part of a club is meeting new people and not so much its actual function.

GIRLS, GIRLS, GIRLS

I wish I knew how hard it was going to be to live with other girls. Every year I've lived in suite style housing so I have always lived with at least six other girls. Growing up I was the only girl in my house besides my mom and never had to deal with the drama and personality clashes that come with living in the same small space with other females. It is extremely difficult, when your living situation is bad, to have anything else go smoothly. My room and my roommates are part of every day and anytime we had issues it seemed as though everything else on my to-do list was ten times more stressful. I wish I knew how challenging it was going to be.

LIKE MOTHER LIKE SON

I wish I knew that sometimes I was going to act like a parent. The roommate experience was the most surprising. Having to deal with other people who weren't my family was very different. Sharing a living space and a bathroom was rough. It was strange to have to argue with people to clean up after themselves. I'd come home after class and find piles of dishes in my sink. The smell of old food was the norm in our kitchen. **I felt like my mom at times,** yelling at my roommates to put the dishes away and clean up after themselves.

I wish I knew I didn't have to buy EVERY dorm room accessory when shopping for freshman year.

STUCK TO ROOMMATES

I wish I knew my roommates did not have to be my best friends. I had heard this before but it didn't click for me until about a month into first semester. We all got along well the first week, but once everyone's true selves started to show, there were problems. When we first moved in everyone was nervous to make friends. Everyone put on a good face and it was as if we became best friends in minutes.

Don't get me wrong I am glad that I established good friendly relations with my roommates; it made a positive living environment. The only problem was that when something bugged me or we got on each other's nerves about something we had nobody else to run to. I wish I had found other friends to hang out with early on in the year so that I wasn't stuck being around people that I didn't get along with all the time.

I wish I knew that "sexiling" was a real thing. I can't count the number of times I came back to my room at night and couldn't get in because of the sock on the door handle.

DEALING WITH DIFFERENCES

I wish I knew how to deal with the differences in people. I came from a small town where we have all known each other from the age of four years old. My class consisted of only 80-90 students and we were all, for the most part, very similar. We all had the same style of clothing and all acted alike. Being placed freshman year with random people allowed me to realize that not everyone is the same. One of my roommates was very different and learning to accept her differences and get along with her was not easy. In general, **having to share space and compromise with other people took time.**

As time goes on you learn to deal with certain people and certain habits so in the end you are able to work it out and live together. However, I wish I was more prepared in living with people who were more diverse than I am.

DORM BUBBLE

I wish I knew that my dorm room was not a bubble. What I mean by that is that even though my key was the only key that opens my room it doesn't mean the room was just mine. When I first came to school I was so excited about my privacy. Unfortunately I let it get to my head. I would keep bottles of alcohol in my room, even though I was underage, and acted completely as if the room was my bubble. I drew on my walls and didn't even think twice when I accidently broke my desk. Yes it is common sense that the room belongs to the college and it is in fact their property but at seventeen years old, first time living away from home, I felt like the privacy was all mine. Security came into my room one night because I was an idiot.

A girl that I bought alcohol for one night got so drunk that she had to be taken to the hospital. When security questioned her as to where she got the alcohol she told them my name. Sure enough they came knocking on my door and within seconds had used their master key to open up my room and come on in. Aside from the fact that I had provided an underage girl with alcohol

I had liquor bottles all around my room and the drawings around my walls were in clear sight. **I got taken down to security and the rest is history.**

ADJUSTING

I wish I knew that college is not some huge change. When you get to college you will have to figure out a few things for sure but it is not a big deal. My biggest adjustments were the bathroom, privacy, and laundry. Sharing bathrooms is one adjustment you will definitely have to get used to. It is nothing like sharing a bathroom with your brother or sister. There is really no privacy in your room or anywhere else for that matter. Doing laundry can be a real shocker but as long as you don't wait until it smells, as my roommate does on occasion, then it doesn't take much effort. Adjusting is inevitable. For me it was those three aspects but for different people is will be different things. **Be ready to adjust; be ready to compromise.**

I wish I knew I had to defrost my mini-fridge before going on break. I came back to a moldy fridge and a smelly room.

ANTI-ROOMMATE

I wish I knew how hard it was going to be to make friends if you don't like your roommates. My freshman year was awful because I didn't like my roommates and I never got involved in any clubs or organizations on campus. Yes, that makes me sound like a pretty big loser but wait... it gets better. As I watched the girls in my building all hang out with their roommates, walk to class together, eat meals together and party together I was hanging out in my room by myself. Loser with a capital "L."

I didn't like my roommates and all the other girls in my hall already had friends. Everyone says college isn't cliquey but when you are by yourself and everyone else hangs out with groups of friends it isn't easy to squeeze yourself in. **It definitely brought me out of my comfort zone** to meet new girls to hang out with. I am so happy I didn't settle to be friends with only the first girls I met. I was miserable sitting alone in my room some nights but if I had tagged along with my roommate I would have been miserable all year. I also would have never met the great friends I have now.

BACKPACKS

I wish I knew it was acceptable to wear a backpack while walking to class. Before college I made my mom buy me an expensive, trendy bag to carry my books in. Little did I know that it was cool to walk around campus with a backpack.

I wish I knew to bring an umbrella, rain coat and rain boots.

COOL PAJAMAS

I wish I knew that nobody cares about your pajamas. In preparing to go to college I spent a lot of quality shopping time with my mom. There was always an excuse to go buy something for college. I got things for my room, school supplies, clothes and pajamas. I dragged my mom all over the mall looking for the cutest pajamas because I had to look good incase people saw me at night. After walking in and out of stores I finally found the best pajamas. Unfortunately, for the entire outfit it was going to cost me $100. My mom caved and bought them because I, "neeeeeeeded them!" I got a cute tank top, matching pants all the way down to matching slippers. Although having new pajamas is always nice, I was a little excessive.

My first night at school I put on my matching set that I thought about so much and then turned around to see that everyone else was wearing old t-shirts and sweatshirts. I was so disappointed. Nobody even noticed my cute outfit. What a waste of money. **I wish I knew that no one cares about your pajamas.**

MY SHIRT

I wish I knew how to say "no" when a friend wanted to borrow something. Living in a dorm of all girls was like having a massive sleep over. Very quickly girls began sharing clothes and accessories. It became so natural for one girl to ask another girl to borrow something with the assumption that they could. I, on the other hand, was not one to share. I learned about sharing when I was young and I am good at it but when it comes to *my* clothes, *my* makeup and *my* jewelry I'd rather not share. I've seen girls borrow tops from other girls and at the end of the night be covered in drinks that were spilled on them or food that missed their mouths and dropped in their lap.

I tried to stay away from asking to borrow stuff because I didn't want to be put in the situation of somebody asking me for something. I dreaded the night a friend would ask to borrow something. Sure enough within a few weeks at school it happened. My roommate was stressing because she couldn't find anything to wear. She comes over and says that she wants to look through my clothes because she needs to change it up. I said, "okay" hoping she wouldn't find anything. Within seconds she was trying on shirts and a minute later she says, "I love this!" and **then the dreaded question… "Can I wear this tonight?"** It happened. She asked. What did I do? I caved. I said, "sure but please try and keep it clean it is one of my favorite shirts." I lied. It wasn't my favorite. But it was *mine*.

We went out and all I did was watch her. I was so caught up in the fact that she was wearing my shirt and I didn't want it to get ruined that I wasn't able to enjoy my night. Nothing happened to it. I watched and watched and no drinks ever fell and no food ever slipped. At the end of the night the shirt was fine. Even though nothing happened to it I stressed so much about it. Either I should loosen up a little; I mean it is just a shirt. Or I should have learned how to approach the situation. I wish I knew how to say no when a friend asked to borrow something.

I wish I knew to bring a robe to school. You never know when there might be a fire drill and in case one happens while you're in the shower it's better to be standing outside in your robe than in just a towel.

TOO MUCH CLOTHES

I wish I knew not to pack my entire wardrobe. There is NOT enough room in your dorm for all of your clothes. Before freshman year I probably spent the entire summer slowly packing for school. I was excited and nervous so putting together outfits and packing clothes over the entirety of the summer helped make the transition easier for me. Even though I only wore two or three pairs of the shorts that I owned I liked all of the shorts in my drawer and said the typical, "I'm sure I'll wear these one time," and I packed them. Well, I did that with just about everything I owned.

Even though the northeast gets cold in the winter I was going to school in the middle of August and the sun is still shining for a few months before it gets cold. But, I *had* to bring my winter clothes. What happens if one night it gets really cold? What if everyone wears jeans out one night and I'm the only person with shorts? **I needed everything... or so I thought. Big mistake!**

As I was moving into my room on the first day of college I was just about half way through my boxes and boxes of clothes when I realized I had no more closet space and the extra drawers I brought weren't going to fit. I re-evaluated all of the clothing that I brought. I put some back in boxes to send home with my mom and dad and I packed up some winter clothes that I really wouldn't wear until at least the end of October. Even worse than the clothes that I brought were all of the shoes and the bags that I packed. Why did I bring all of them??? First off there was no room for all of them, secondly I hardly wore half of the shoes that I brought and realistically I use only one bag to hold all of my stuff. I never changed purses when I was home, what made me think I was all of a sudden going to change them daily now? Maybe I thought I was going to reinvent myself and be a cool new college girl. That lasted until the end of move in day when I sent my parents home with 1/3 of the stuff that I had brought.

As the school year went on I realized that aside from my weekend outfits and the business attire I had, my daily choice of clothing was sweatpants and sweatshirts. When I went home for Thanksgiving I packed a box of summer clothes to bring home and exchanged them for a box of winter clothes. There is no need and no way that you can pick up your entire room from home and bring it to college. You quickly learn to be a simpler person than what you were. With too much stuff life will be tough.

I wish I knew not to wait an entire month to do my laundry.

NASTY BATHROOMS

I wish I knew that girls can leave the bathroom just as disgusting as boys. As a freshman I used a common bathroom that the entire hallway of girls used. It had multiple showers, sinks and stalls. There was even a woman who would clean the bathroom for us every day…except the weekends.

Friday night it began. Girls were constantly in and out of the bathroom taking showers, doing their hair or putting on makeup. Even after just ten girls taking a shower and drying their hair there was hair all over the shower drains and sinks. On a Friday or Saturday night there were about fifty girls getting ready to go out. The amount of hair was just a minimal part of the mess. After going out for a night of partying the bathroom was a disaster. There was throw up in the toilets, sometimes on or around the toilets and even sometimes in the sinks. The toilets got clogged at least once each weekend. Even worse than that were the random things like thongs and condoms that ended up in shower stalls. Seriously girls!?!

I wish I knew to bring a pair of flip-flops just to wear in the shower.

PART III

SOCIAL

PARTIES

DATING

LIVING ON YOUR OWN

I wish I knew how easy and fun it was to live on your own. Before attending college I thought it was going to be hard to manage school work and other daily routines and responsibilities. When I came to college I was amazed at how quickly I became acclimated. When you have a ton of responsibilities and nobody to tell you how to tackle them **you begin to really learn about yourself.** Some of my friends found every day to be a challenge. I took it day by day and it got easier and easier. Keep hold of everything you have to do and things will begin to fall into place.

TOO MUCH FREE TIME

I wish I knew how much of a challenge it would be adjusting to the new environment. I knew college would be different but I never expected to be as homesick as I was. I had so much free time and I didn't know how to use it, so I found myself thinking about home. It wasn't until I started getting involved on campus that I finally realized what the problem was. I had too much free time and I needed to fill that space in order to adjust to college life. I had to join clubs, study more, and grab leadership opportunities. My shy personality needed to change in order to get the most out of my school. I had to learn to break out of my shell and take risks.

Now, I am still shy at first and generally quiet but I'm better at realizing that. I am in a various number of clubs and organization and I can't imagine life at college without them. I have learned to adapt to a new environment, manage my time and take advantage of the opportunities put before me.

NEVER ENDING ALCOHOL

I wish I knew that the supply of alcohol doesn't run out at college parties. In high school when I went to a party, I drank the way that most of my friends drank; I drank until there was no more alcohol left. I filled a water bottle up half way with vodka I stole from my parent's liquor cabinet. I went to the party, finish the water bottle and then the rest of the night I ran around with my friends to see who had a little bit of alcohol left to share. This usually left me with a few hours at the end of the night to enjoy myself and be a little crazy with my friends. In college there is never really a time when the alcohol runs out.

In college people buy entire handles, maybe even two or three and who knows, if they're feeling like it's going to be a good night they may add on some beer for the night as well. Now the problem is that when I was in high school I drank what I had, so when I got to college I still tried to drink what I had. Well when there is alcohol in front of you the entire night, **it is inevitable that more than once your night will end badly**; especially freshman year. You don't realize your tolerance and you very easily lose track of how much you actually drink. I started holding a marker in my bag when I went out. Every time I had a drink I would put a tally mark on my forearm. For the first night I did it I was at five tally marks before I even knew it. This was well before my night had ended so I can only imagine how much I was drinking before I started this new tally system.

If someone would have told me how accessible alcohol was in college I would have been much more aware of my drinking. I loved parties in high school because what I thought was being drunk was actually just being buzzed. I didn't really learn what being drunk was until I got to college. I wasn't an alcoholic but some nights I even questioned my drinking habits. Often times freshman year I didn't remember every part of my night and when all I wanted to do was go to sleep I couldn't because the room didn't stop spinning.

In high school those fun morning hangovers at the deli where I talked with friends about the night before turned into terrible day long hangovers at college where all I did was stay in bed and watch TV. Thankfully, as soon as I started tallying my drinks I was having the best nights at college. I was drinking with my friends and I got a better idea of how much a certain amount of alcohol affected me. I was enjoying my nights and I loved every bit of college.

NO LONGER AN ATHLETE

I wish I knew how hard it was going to be to *not* be an athlete. Being an athlete in high school was my identity. All of my friends new me as an athlete, my room had pictures of my championship teams, trophies and medals all around. My typical day was school, practice and then possible another practice for my club team. Being an athlete was my identity.

I was recruited to be an athlete in college but I choose not to. I figured I wanted to experience college in a different way. I wanted to do things in college that I wasn't able to do in high school. When I came to college I had a great time partying with friends, sleeping in on the weekends and working out in the gym on my own time. Unfortunately because I wasn't playing a sport I realized I was just a student and nothing more. I had lost my identity. My new friends looked at me differently than all my friends in high school looked at me. I no longer stood out for being a top athlete. **I didn't know what my identity was anymore.**

I used the next few months to try out as many clubs and organizations at my school. I dabbled in a few before I found where I was most comfortable. I got a job on campus and began to take advantage of the free time I had. I made a point to befriend some of the athletes at my school. Many of my friends in high school played sports and the current friends I had at college were the farthest thing from athletes. I found that I actually had more in common with my new friends that I met than the friends I had for the first few years of college. It was important to find at least one solid good friend. My sport was my stability throughout my life. In college when I didn't have it I felt like something was missing. I felt like I didn't have anything stable or constant throughout my life. Finding that great friend added more of what my life was missing. I continued to work hard to prove to myself that I could handle life on my own; that I could handle life without being an athlete.

To this day I still have a hard time identifying myself. My sport was who I was for the majority of my life. Today there isn't one aspect that makes me who I am. I am a mixture of a lot of little things from my school. **Don't lose sight of who you are.** Your sport may take up your life in high school so brainstorm the new things you plan on doing when you get to college if you aren't going to be playing a sport. Create your new identity in college.

WALK OF SHAME

I wish I knew that the walk of shame really happens. It happens to many, many girls. I used to get up around 5:30am to go to practice some mornings. One of the greatest things to see was a girl, holding her shoes, still wearing the clothes she was wearing the night before, walking down the road to her dorm. Girls, just so you know, wearing an oversized sweatshirt that you took from the guys room to walk back to your dorm doesn't hide the fact that you are walking a walk of shame. Just because your head is hidden by the sweatshirt hood it is still 5:30am, you are still holding your shoes which usually look like shoes a stripper would wear, and by the swagger in your walk I'm assuming you are still drunk. That sweatshirt is so big that it covers your mini skirt so much that it looks like you aren't even wearing pants. Enjoy your hangover. Enjoy that feeling of guilt. Oh yes, there is no way you can hide the walk of shame.

GO GET LIFE

I wish I knew college life would not come to me; I would have to go to it. It was so important to branch out and socialize the first two weeks. It definitely does take you out of your comfort zone but two awkward weeks pays off big for the next four years.

LEAVING YOUR COMFORT ZONE

I wish I knew that the whole experience of college will take you out of your comfort zone and open you up to tons of new things. Moving away from home and your parents, meeting new people, taking all kinds of classes, it's just a time full of changes. All of these changes may seem overwhelming, but you learn to adapt and you realize all of the changes are for the better. My sophomore year was full of new experiences.

On the first day of classes, I woke up at four in the morning to stand on line and secure my spot to go study abroad for the second semester. I wasn't even sure of my decision at that point – 5 months in a foreign country without my family and friends and at a whole new school – I was overwhelmed. But I did it, and I'm so glad I did. I took myself out of my comfort zone, meeting new people, living in a new place, and taking classes in a different country. It wasn't easy as first but once I adapted and embraced the changes, I knew I was in for a great experience. College opens you up to so many great things, but it's up to you to step out of your comfort zone and see what they're all about.

USED TO BE
AN ATHLETE

I wish I knew how hard it was going to be not being able to play a sport. I was an all-conference three sport athlete in high school. My senior year I was unable to play soccer and basketball due to a torn ACL and meniscus. I was devastated when it happened. Even worse than the fact it happened was that now all of the colleges that were looking to scout me stopped scouting me because I was unable to play.

While all of my friends were getting letters asking them to come visit colleges and meet with coaches I was doing research, like the majority of other students, on colleges that I wanted to go visit. All of my friends had committed to play sports at colleges in the beginning of our senior year. As they enjoyed playing their sports and relaxing on the weekends I was out with my parents traveling to schools to take campus tours and do admissions interviews. I went through the application process and checked my mailbox every day until I got accepted, the normal way. Once I got my acceptance letters I finally decided on a college that I liked. Unfortunately no matter how much I liked the college I would never be an athlete again. I thought that I could handle the fact that I could now restart my image and be somebody other than an athlete. I was completely wrong.

I never, even to this day, have found the support system even close to what I had when I was on my basketball or soccer teams. I wish somebody would have given me the heads up that it wouldn't be easy to be a normal student.

STUDYING ABROAD

I wish I knew to try as many different things in college as I could. I say this because of my experience studying abroad. If I knew that every new thing I tried, even if it seemed scary or intimidating, would be as good as my study abroad experience I would have participated in more activities, joined more clubs, and met as many people as I could. **Studying abroad was the best experience of my life.**

I went by myself to the other side of the world hoping to gain a greater perspective and experience. What I got in return by the end of the five months was a new family of other students in my program, a lot of once-in-a lifetime experiences and greater independence. I felt like I grew as a person and came back with a new point of view of the world. Although somewhat scary, I took the opportunity to travel across the world and live life differently for five months. It was the best experience of my life and I am so grateful that I took advantage of that opportunity. You never know how one moment or event may affect the rest of your life.

FREE TIME

I wish I knew how much free time I would have. Before coming to college I never put any effort into my homework or classes. I would never study or put more effort than needed into the work I did. Then, arriving at college I was presented with more free time than ever before. Instead of being in school for six hours I was only in class three hours of the day and some days I didn't even have class. I was then given homework assignments that weren't due for a week or two. In addition to that I was presented with people constantly being around and there were options to party every night of the week. Suddenly, no one was there to make me do homework. Drinking a beer with the guys or throwing a party took priority in my life. **If I could have done anything better in high school I would have learned motivation and destroyed the procrastination skills I had developed.** Catching up on work was always a nightmare and it taught me to be more responsible.

DON'T BE SOMETHING YOU'RE NOT

I wish I knew not to be afraid to be myself and do whatever it is I enjoy most. College is much different than high school and middle school. People come from many different backgrounds, cultures and regions. Everyone's interests are different. In college, people are much more accepting and the level of peer pressure is much lower. In my experience, I have met so many wonderful people and **I have never felt the need to be something I am not.**

College is the time for you to branch out, discover new things and find out what you enjoy doing most. It is an exciting time full of exciting opportunities. Never do something just because someone else is. You will be much happier investing time in things you truly enjoy. I tell you that from experience.

Take advantage of opportunities you find important and you will enter and leave college feeling accomplished. Everything I have told you is what I did and thought about from the start. I wouldn't trade my experiences for anything.

ME TIME

I wish I knew I would never be alone. I didn't realize that I would not only have to set aside time for me to do my work but I would also have to set aside time for just myself. Earlier this year I had become extremely stressed and was slowly become depressed. Before it got worse I reached out to a friend who was older for some advice. She told me that **regardless of how much work I had that day or what was on my mind that I should find time for me and only me**. It was hard to do at first. I was always surrounded by people. Some days when I was really overwhelmed and missed my family I would feel even lonelier. At college even when you feel lonely, you are never really alone. There is always something going on and there are always people around.

I made a point to grab my headphones and walk around campus whenever I got stressed. This helped to block out other noises. It also gave me some alone time. No friends around and no work to stress about; I had found me time. The simple act of walking around campus made a drastic drop in my stress level. I got away from everything and was able to put my day and my tasks into perspective. I wish I knew that no matter how overwhelmed, stressed, or lonely I would feel I would never really be alone. I wish I knew the benefits of making "me" time before I had gotten to the point of being depressed.

NO THANKS SOCIAL SCENE

I wish I knew what the social night scene was before I came to college. Loud music, clubs, and lots of alcohol are not on my list of favorite things to do.

NO CLIQUES

I wish I knew that most people at college are friendly for the most part and groups of people don't form "cliques" as they did in high school. You know what group of friends people hang out with but there are so many people at college that you won't find the stereotypically cliques from high school. This would have been good to know because I wouldn't have spent so much time being worried and nervous to make friends or finding the right people to hang out with.

"GOING OUT" CLOTHES

I wish I knew that people went out to clubs and parties way more in college than they did in high school. If I would have known this I would have definitely packed more clothes to go out in. I think most girls don't realize this either and run out of their "going out" clothes after only a few weeks. After the first month we all needed some new clubbing clothes. I didn't want to spend a ton of money on clothes because I knew that after a night of partying it was inevitable that shirts, skirts and dresses would be ruined. Ruined from alcohol, food, or on a hard night of drinking maybe even throw up.

My friends and I would go to really cheap clothes stores to buy outfits to party in. Sure enough the majority of clothes we bought only lasted a semester. They always got ruined. We didn't care. The clothes I bought I planned to throw out at the end of the semester anyway. There was no way I was bringing those clothes home; I never wanted my parents to see what I was actually wearing.

NO "I" IN TEAM

I wish I knew how much I would miss playing a competitive sport. I always used to get my exercise from school sports but now that I'm not playing I've learned that I have to find my own time and create my own workouts to get myself in shape. When I was looking at college I was okay with not playing a sport in college. Every school that I looked at had either club teams or intramural teams. I chose a school that had an active intramural sports program thinking it was going to be like playing a high school sport. I quickly learned intramural sports were not at all like high school sports.

Intramural sports never gave me the same feelings or activities as playing in high school. The team we formed did not at all feel like the team I had in high school. We didn't have practices and we had so many people on the team that if somebody didn't want to show up they didn't have to. Another thing is that we formed our team with our group of friends. **The fun thing was I was with my friends. The not so fun thing was not all of my friends were athletic.** They would come to games to have a good time and to check out the girls. It was so frustrating playing with a bunch of guys who had no idea what they were doing. There was also no coach to yell at them or tell them to pick it up. I used to love playing hard and impressing my coaches in high school. Now I had nobody to impress and nobody to give me advice to make me better. I wish I knew all of this before coming to college so that my hopes would not have been so high thinking I would still be able to play a team sport.

I DON'T DRINK

I wish I knew that you can still make friends in college even if you don't drink alcohol. When I first came to college the one thing I was most nervous about was the fact that I didn't drink. In high school my friends didn't care that I didn't drink but they never invited me out to parties because of it. If they did invite me out I knew it was just because they wanted me to drive. When they started to party a lot more our friendships started to grow apart. I was pretty worried this would happen in college too.

To my surprise, when I got here, no one cared. They would be getting dressed to go out at night and I would just sit on the couch. One night when they were getting ready they asked me why I wasn't getting dressed. I said, "I don't drink." They looked at me, and almost in unison said, "So? Come with us anyway." It was such an awesome feeling knowing they wanted me to come even though I wasn't drinking.

Today, as a senior I still live with those same guys. I realized that I was limiting my friendships because I was so worried about the fact that I didn't drink. My friends are awesome and **friendships in college aren't all about drinking** and partying together. I couldn't have asked for better friends.

NICE SORORITIES

I wish I knew that many (but not all) sororities and fraternities are not how they appear in the movies. As a freshman, I decided not to go out for a sorority because I thought the girls were going to be mean, make me do things I didn't want to do, and I would only be allowed to be friends with the girls in the sorority. After seeing some of my friends join and finding out that the sororities on my campus are not like I imagined, I decided to join. I now love everyone in my sorority and I have ample time to do other things outside of it. I regret not joining my freshman year just because I was scared. I feel like I missed out on a year. I wish someone would have told me to try things I am interested in. I would have realized sooner what I liked and if I didn't like it, well **nothing is written in stone.**

LEARNING FROM EXPERIENCE

I wish I knew how much I would learn about life. I have learned a ton about myself, what makes me happy and what I need to do in my life. College has taught me so much about my life. I have learned many life lessons and a lot about being an adult. I learned more from the college experience than I have from the college classroom.

I wish I knew that there are a lot of kids in college who never drank in high school. I always thought I was going to be the only one.

HANGOVER CURE

I wish I knew that I would have to take preventative measures to lessen my hangover in college. In high school I drank, woke up with a headache and went on with my day. In college I drank, woke up with a headache, the spins, sweating, and nauseous, on an easy day. I soon learned that I need to chug a couple bottles of water before bed after a night of drinking and partying. Everyone learns a trick to curing a hangover. For me, it's any food covered in grease.

NAPS

I wish I knew how much I was going to nap in college. I have never napped before going to college but as soon as I got there I started napping once a day almost every day of the week. A lot of time it would be during the normal school day. I would come back after class, lay in my bed, which by the way was way more comfortable than my bed at home because I had so many pillows and doubled up on mattress pads that I would just fall right asleep. Sometimes **on the weekends**

my friends and I would take power naps after dinner to prepare for a long night of going out. Now as a junior I have a lot of others things going on during my day than when I was a freshman but I still make sure to find time to take my nap.

I wish I knew how different college parties would be compared to high school parties. Wow!

HOW TO GET A GIRLFRIEND

I wish I knew more about girl's emotions. I saw, on a daily basis, girls crying because they missed their parents or boyfriend. At first it took me by surprise. I went around trying to find the hottest girls and unfortunately they all had boyfriends. Their boyfriends were all from home, so I made it my job to break them up. No I'm just kidding!

What I did do was be their friend. Eventually the majority of girls do break up with their boyfriends and then that's the time to pounce. When you finally find a girl without a boyfriend, hold on to them because they don't come that often.

In high school I was a jock and hung out with most of the more popular kids. That was enough to impress girls. But college is a whole new experience; I needed to find new ways to impress girls. I chose the funny guy route, and trust me all girls love a guy who is funny. Girls stress in college. They stress because they miss their parents, they miss their friends from home, they miss their boyfriends or they are upset because of typical girl drama. If you can make them laugh, you can make their day. That's how I got my girlfriend.

ONCE A TOUGH GUY
TWICE A LOSER

I wish I knew not to be a tough guy. In high school I was a jock, I always worked out, and getting girls was pretty easy. I was so excited to go to school because I couldn't wait to get with as many girls as I could. When I was packing my bags for college I made sure to sneak in a couple of handles of liquor. The first day I got there I was pretty pumped because my roommate seemed normal. Our parents left, I reached into my bag, pulled out my handle and said, "Here's to a good year. Let's get some tonight." My roommate didn't seem like the type to go out hard but he decided to join in the fun. **The first few weekends I always brought home a girl.** Many of them were bombs, but hey I still got some. I was focusing on quantity, not quality. Over the first semester I continued to do what I did every weekend. It ended up backfiring badly.

I used to be a jock. I used to be ripped. I was now focused so much on partying that I hardly went to the gym and my six pack abs was now a gut. Needless to say second semester was quite different. I didn't have the confidence I had going into first semester and I think girls got the hint I was looking for anything but a girlfriend. I definitely had too much of a good thing. I watched my roommate who now had a steady girlfriend. He always seemed happy and he always had a good night out. He never had to use any game and he still got laid. I now had a gut and the girls that I was hooking up with were onto the next guys. Any girl who I met knew my name. I definitely had a bad reputation at that point. I wish I knew the benefits of being a tough guy weren't worth it and would easily run out.

I wish I knew boys aren't ready for relationships until their "single life" is out of their system.

RELATIONSHIPS HAPPEN IN A MINUTE

I wish I knew that there is really no dating phase in college relationships. I guess there really is no dating phase in high school relationships either but at least in high school after I hung out with a guy I went home to my own house at night. At my college there are no rules about guys and girls being in each other rooms. As long as it's okay with your roommate, a guy can sleep over a girl's room and vice versa.

I met a guy that I liked. I saw him all the time. We would hang out on the weekends together but with all of our friends. People tend to travel in packs. It was hard to get away from my friends to be with the guy I was interested in. I wouldn't consider getting a meal at the dining hall a date. We were spending so much time together that after a week we were basically a couple. Our friends treated us like a couple and we were only hooking up with each other so why not be a couple? It happens to fast.

If you're interesting in a guy and he is interested in you it can easily become messy unless you talk about what kind of relationship you want to have. Stay friends? Only hook up? Relationships happen fast and if you don't communicate about what you want, you may find yourself in a situation where you're going to have to "break up" with somebody just to stop hooking up with them.

GIRLFRIEND FROM HOME, NO MORE

I wish I knew how tough it was to have a relationship and maintain that relationship. Many freshman girls like to hook up with guys and many guys like to make use of the opportunity to have a little fun without being in a relationship. When I first came to college I was in a relationship with a girl from home. It was hard for a couple of reasons. The first being that the girls at college were looking for a fun time and the only fun I could have was to look at them. My other friends, who didn't have girlfriends, were having the time of their lives. Going out, partying and hooking up with all kinds of girls. Often times I had to go back home to see my girlfriend and I would miss out on weekends with my friends from school. Needless to say, I quickly ended that relationship.

Now I am in a relationship with a girl who goes to the same school as me. It is one million times better because she is here and can hang out with my group of friends. I no longer have to worry about going home and missing out on the fun at college. Freshman year was the best year of my life regardless but the fun really came after I broke up with my girlfriend from home and took advantage of the opportunity to meet other girls at my school.

BOYFRIEND GOT IN THE WAY

I wish I knew how much I could actually mature and better myself. From the time I was in middle school I have always been in a relationship. Not knowing it could last as long as it did I dated the same guy from my freshman year of high school all the way to when I was in college. There were break ups here and there and a handful of rough patches but back then I didn't know any better and was overwhelmed with the simple fact of having a boyfriend. Having a boyfriend didn't mess with my grades all that much but it sure changed a lot about who I was and who I could have been. All my friends were the type to always go out and drink, hang out with boys and find ways to "have fun." However, because I had a boyfriend I was always with him. It wasn't a healthy relationship. There was more jealousy and control than there was love and comfort. As I got older and wanted a boyfriend less and less **I realized the person I was was not the person I wanted to be.** The people I was hanging out with were not the people I wanted to associate myself with.

By the end of my freshman year of college I was on the right track to be the person I wanted to be. I was on the track to becoming the person I knew I really was. I broke up with my boyfriend and I decided I didn't want any guy in my life for a while, considering I just had to deal with one for over five years. I eventually got closer with my friends, doing my own thing and felt better about myself every day. Then out of the blue over the summer I fell in love. When I wasn't looking for a boyfriend or even thinking about a boyfriend he showed up. He came into my life when I was comfortable with who I was and when I was living my life for me. He just fit right in.

I wish I knew that I had the potential to find out who I was when I went to college. I was so caught up with guys that it blurred my own vision of myself. Now that I know who I am, I am happy with whom I am and I have a boyfriend who loves me for the right reasons. I couldn't be happier. I learned who was important in my life, who wasn't, who took advantage of me and who didn't.

LONG DISTANCE RELATIONSHIPS

I wish I knew that having a girlfriend at another college wasn't that bad at all. My girlfriend and I dated all of our senior year of high school. Like many couples, we talked about what we were going to do in college. We both agreed that it wouldn't be a good idea to go to the same college. Not because we wanted to meet other people but we knew it was important that we focus on ourselves and grow as individuals. It all sounded great in theory but when we actually committed to different colleges reality hit. We had to have the discussion about deciding whether to actually keep our relationship going or go our separate ways. After talking, and many tears later, we decided that being in two different places wasn't an excuse to end a relationship. We planned on staying together, despite what other friends said about relationships like ours never lasting.

It was hard saying goodbye to her but it ended up not being as bad as I thought. With her at a different school is gave me opportunities to meet guys and spend a lot of time with them. The time that we had at our own schools gave us the opportunity to form excellent friendships. She has some of the best friends she has ever made and **I couldn't ask for better friends at my school**. I also don't have to deal with drunken hook ups and messy drunk girls the way that some of my friends did. Seeing some of the girls at my college made me a little nervous as to what kinds of girls may be influencing my girlfriend at her school. On the other hand, I trusted my girlfriend. We would never hide anything from each other and we talked every day. Today I am a junior and I am still with the same girlfriend. Things have been great. If the love is there and people are trustworthy, keeping a long distance relationship, even in college can be done.

"MARRIED" TO MY GIRLFRIEND

I wish I knew how easy it was for relationships to get out of hand at college. I have had girlfriends in the past but college relationships are a different story. When I first got here I met a girl and we were just hooking up every once in a while, no big deal it was just for fun. As time went on it got more serious and we started to hang out more and more. Eventually by the end of the first year we couldn't leave each other's side. Now, this sounds like a typical boyfriend-girlfriend situation in college right? Wrong!? The second year rolled around and we were still fine but still not "official." That got her mad for sure. Then we started to have sleepovers. A sleepover here and there wasn't bad but after a month it turned into a sleepover every single night. It was ridiculous to say the least. She would get paranoid that if she didn't sleep with me I would sleep somewhere else or with someone else. This isn't like being home where you can go to each other's house and the parents make you sit on the couch and then leave at night. The girls and guys can stay in your room like it's not a big deal. Anyway, now as a junior it is like we are married. She sleeps over every single night, we go food shopping together, she buys me clothes, does my laundry, I cook for her, rent movies, do homework, everything, just like a married couple. Don't tell her but...I'm breaking up with her tonight.

GIRLFRIEND THERE FRIENDS HERE

I wish I knew how to balance life with a girlfriend at another college. A lot of people think that you need to break up with your girlfriend from high school when you go to college. I had a great girlfriend in high school and we decided to stay together when we went to college. I think it was a great idea, except for a few things. I wish I knew how to balance the time with my girlfriend at another school and my friends at the college I'm at now.

Some nights I wouldn't go out with all the guys because I would stay in to talk to my girlfriend. My girlfriend never begged me to stay in my dorm and talk to her. I loved talking to her I just couldn't find a good balance between talking to her and going out with my friends. I wish we had discussed more about how we would communicate in college while we were still in high school. There should have been a much better balance between my girlfriend and my friends.

DEEP RELATIONSHIPS

I wish I knew how much better and deeper relationships are formed in college. If I had known this beforehand **I wouldn't have sweat all the high school drama.** I had a boyfriend throughout high school who I loved. He wasn't only my boyfriend but he was my best friend. When we broke up, during our senior year, I felt like it was the end of the world. We broke up because life was changing; we were headed to two different colleges.

I think I was so used to having a boyfriend in high school that when I got to college it only took a few weeks until I met a new guy. I was amazed at the fact that we have an even stronger relationship than the one I had with my high school boyfriend. I wish I knew how different, for the better, my relationship would be in college. If I knew there was better ahead of me I wouldn't have let my high school break up affect me the way it did. I would have definitely been upset but I think I would have appreciated the fun times we had together rather than worry that I would be alone for the rest of my life. I wish I had known that the world of relationships was bigger than what was inside the walls of my high school.

FRESHMAN BOYS

I wish I knew how much boys tried to be players during freshman year. Watch out! The key word here is tried. See, all boys aren't players but when one boy says he is his friends' competitive nature will come out and try to out play him. Eventually it becomes a domino effect and the majority of freshman boys will work on trying to get with the most girls. It becomes a competitive thing. Who can get with the most girls each weekend, each semester, and each year? Don't let a guy play you.

Like I said, not all of them are actually players and a lot of the good guys don't shine through for a few weeks. Let the players get it out of their system because for many of them the desire to be a player dies down as the year goes on. When that desire wears off that's when you find the good guys. Give it some time and don't be one of the girls who are easily played. I have self respect and I never let a guy play me. It took about a month for the good guys to shine through. While all of my friends were complaining because they couldn't find a nice guy I was patient and waited to find one of the few guys who were actually a keeper. It's been three years and we're still together.

PART IV

SCHOOL WORK

PROFESSORS

CLASSROOM

PAY ATTENTION IN HIGH SCHOOL

I wish I knew that what I was learning in my high school classes I would use in my college classes. I never liked my science classes. I like the subject of science, I thought it was all fascinating but I never liked studying for my classes or taking tests on it. I was planning on studying business in college so in high school it was natural to hear me say in a science class, "I'm going to be a business student in college so these science classes don't even matter." Well let me tell you…it's called the core curriculum, a.k.a. general education credits and yes, those science classes do matter.

Many colleges have them and they are liberal arts based courses including math, English, sciences, arts etc. that all students must complete. Even though I was a business student I still had to fulfill those credits. Since I disliked science so much I decided to put it off until my senior year schedule. Then as a senior, I took a 100 level biology course for non-science majors. It seemed harmless. I figured I would fly through it with the rest of the non-science majors since it was basic material. So basic in fact that it was almost exactly the same information as I had learned in my high school biology class. Here are the problems: (A) I didn't pay attention in my high school biology class and (B) I was four years out of high school already that I couldn't remember anything anyway. I wish I had just paid attention in high school and taken the biology course that I had put off for four years when I was a freshman or a sophomore. That way the little that I had learned in high school I would have been able to apply to my college course and I would have been able to get it over with. Instead I sat in my biology course as a senior, studying every weekend, and struggling to maintain a B average.

LIBRARY IS NOW MY BFF

I wish I knew how much time I'd be spending in the library; I'd probably have paid more attention to it on tour. The only time I really used the library at my high school was when one of my teachers held a class there. It was usually a boring class about learning how to research online.

When I went on tours to colleges I hardly paid attention to the library because I figured I would have nothing to do with it. Then I went to college and completely surprised myself. The majority of the work I did I did in the library. My dorm was too noisy. The study lounges in my dorm were steps away from my room and my friends were walking by constantly so naturally I was distracted. I always found some excuse to pack up my work and hang out with my friends. Any time I actually needed to get work done I headed to the library. It was so quiet and had all of the resources I needed. Another nice thing about the library was that when I went there it automatically put me into work mode. This was great because I dedicated that space as my work area. As soon as I stepped out of the library I was able to not think about the work I had to do. I actually put library time in my planner so that I would force myself to go there and get some work done every day. This helped to keep me organized and I never fell behind on my work. The library is now my best friend.

I wish I knew to take college one day at a time. There is a lot of work in college and it is important to prioritize and stay organized.

SO MUCH WRITING

I wish I knew the amount of writing there was going to be in college. Before college I was not prepared for the amounts of essays I would have to write each week. I am not even an English major! If I knew this before coming to college I would have made a point to take more English courses in high school. My school offered some creative writing and college writing courses and if I had taken them I think I would have been way more prepared for all of the writing I am doing now.

STUDY HABITS

I wish I knew how to study. My biggest regret was not studying in high school. I didn't feel the need to study in high school. I was one of those students. The material in class came easy to me. I didn't have to study because the tests were easy and I still was able to maintain A's and B's. Also, exams were only a percentage of my grades. I was able to bring up my grades in high school because of participation points, projects, homework assignments, and in class assignments. Why study, right? Wrong! Even though I didn't necessarily have to put in extra time for my classes in high school I wish I did. **It would have been beneficial to get into a routine** because it was a rude awakening coming to college and not being familiar with how to study. There was no way I could get away with not studying in my classes in college and still get a good grade. The material I was learning in college was taught fast, it was very detailed, and it was difficult. Unlike in high school when teachers give you material to study, you memorize it and then spit it back on the test, in college you need to understand the concepts in order to do well on exams. My professors never gave me problems on an exam that were verbatim to what we had learned.

To this day I am still learning how to study properly. It is so important to be able to study because the majority of my final grades for my courses are based on just three or four exams. I can no longer make a huge impact on my grade by just showing up to class and participating. If I had good study habits from high school I would have been way more prepared for college exams.

NO SLACK

I wish I knew that college was way harder than high school. In high school I could pretty much get away with anything. There are always makeup tests and teachers, for the most part, allow late homework. However, in college I was given an extreme amount of freedom, which is incredibly misleading. Just because I had been given the freedom to do whatever I wanted, whenever I wanted, didn't mean that it wouldn't come back and bite me in the end. Falling behind in my work, even in the slightest bit, only made things harder. **I found myself in over my head before I knew it.**

Besides making that mistake, professors had an extremely limited number of excuses they accepted for missed work. In many cases if a student didn't do the work, too bad. The hardest thing to realize was that I was no longer a child and I had been handed a great deal of responsibility. I was no longer being babied and not doing my work was completely up to me.

Understand that in college you are hardly given any slack. What I liked most is that when I did my work professors noticed and respected that. If I did my work I did well and if I didn't do my work my grade suffered. It is even more gratifying knowing I did it all on my own. I am an adult now. I wish I knew to take advantage of that responsibility and never fall behind.

I wish I knew to keep a balance between work and play.

WORK HARD, PLAY HARD

I wish I knew that it would be brutal to cram for tests the night before. One of the biggest changes from high school to college was unlike high school where I would always cram for tests or do an assignment the night before it was due, I could no longer do it in college. Never before college did I actually think I was going to have to read whole books. In high school I found summaries online of every book I was supposed to read and it was always enough to pass my classes. In college, that doesn't work. English professors ask detailed questions and during class everyone had to participate on the discussion. If I could go back I would start to get into better habits of studying because it would have made my transition a lot less stressful. Unlike in high school, in order to stay in college I have to meet certain grade requirements. If you want to have fun in college you must be willing to work hard to stay there.

SCHOOL WORK HAS TAKEN OVER

I wish I knew what I was getting myself into when I went to college. In high school I loaded up on extracurricular activities, maintained a steady part time job all four years, and played a competitive sport. I convinced myself that I was well prepared for the work load at college because I would no longer be participating in everything I did back home. Little did I know, school work took over my life. I was always told about time management, but it is impossible to predict what your work load will be like at college.

JOB SEARCH

I wish I knew to start job searching as a freshman. College is four years long, why wait until junior or senior year to begin the job search? Yes, as a freshman you may not get the best internship or the best position in a club or organization but at least you get your name and face on the radar. That way when you are a junior and you go back to meet campus recruiters, company representatives, etc. they will know your face over the other hundreds or thousands of juniors trying to get the same job.

The other benefit is that if you begin your job search as a freshman you can get exposed to different careers before you get tied down to one. I wanted to learn more about the hotel industry. After my freshman year I applied for a summer job to work at a hotel front desk. I got the job, I bought the best work outfits, and I was ready to take on the challenge. My first customer service experience was a man who walked up to the front desk and demanded that facilities went to his room because his sink wasn't draining fast enough. "Are you kidding me, I wish I could pour you down a drain right now," is what I thought. "Okay sir, I will send somebody up right away," is what I said. I couldn't believe the man. Who did he think he was? I couldn't deal with people like him so naturally after day two…I quit.

I didn't have a family to support, I didn't have bills to pay and at the end of the summer I was headed back to school so it wasn't as though I would go home, sit on the couch and do nothing for the rest of the my life. Imagine if I had graduated college and that was the job

I got? I would be miserable. I wouldn't be able to quit after two days because at that point I'd have bills to pay and I'd have to begin paying off student loans.

Lucky for me I got that experience while I was young enough to say, "No thanks, what's next?" and then try something different. I wish I had tried more things on campus as a freshman in terms of learning about jobs. If I had gone to guest speakers, went to career talks, etc. I would have learned more about the things I liked and didn't like. Like I said before, I would have also been able to show my face to companies and organizations. That way they would see that I was motivated and proactive about getting a job. I wish I knew to take advantage of the job opportunities even as a freshman.

CHOOSING A MAJOR

I wish I knew what I wanted to do with my life. I wish I had explored all of my options before choosing a major. I just picked a major because it was a subject I enjoyed learning about. I never thought about what types of jobs I could get from it. I should have met with professors to talk about careers options in other fields. I should have done research on job placement for certain majors. I should have talked with upper classmen about what their classes were like and what kinds of opportunities they had. I didn't do any of that and now I am a senior and don't want to do anything with what I've been studying for the last four years of college. **Sorry Mom and Dad.**

FAILING A TEST

I wish I knew that one test failed wasn't going to be the end of my college career. It was my own fault. I didn't study. I went to class and completely bombed my test. I knew I did, even before I got my grade. When my professor finally uploaded the grades online I thought my life was over. I got a 35! How is that even possible right? I managed to get the lowest grade in the class. Maybe there are students who don't stress about this kind of stuff but I am usually a strong student so when I saw the 35 **I was ready to pack my clothes up and head home.**

I stressed for the entire weekend about what was going to happen to me. I sent my professor an e-mail telling him how embarrassed I was and I actually apologized for the horrible grade I received. He didn't e-mail me back right away, which is normal, but of course at that time I figured he was meeting with the Dean of our school and figuring out how to break the news to me that I would be kicked out of school or have to go on academic probation.

The next day when I woke up I saw an e-mail from my professor. I braced myself for the worst. He actually told me not to stress about it. It turns out a lot of the other students in my class struggled as well. He told me it was great that I was so concerned and that he would allow me to do extra credit to help my grade. The rest of the semester I worked so hard that I ended up with a B in the class. Can you believe that? I got a 35 on an exam and I still got a B! I wish somebody told me that if I messed up on an assignment it wasn't the end of my college career. I would have still e-mailed my professor but I definitely wouldn't have stressed as much as I did.

BACK UP

I wish I knew to ALWAYS back up my papers and notes I have on my laptop; an external hard drive in key. Laptops crash at the worst times; the day before exams, right when you finish your paper and even worse, right before finals week.

PICK PERFECT PROFESSORS

I wish I knew that it was more important to register for a class based on who the professor is rather than the time of the class. There are some that will disagree and say that as long as all of their classes don't start until noon they are happy. If that's the case then what I say doesn't matter. However I strongly suggest you do continue reading on.

I used to be the student who scheduled classes based on what time they were and when I finally did some research on professors and based my schedule on the professor rather than the time of the class it turned out to be the best class I had ever taken. Think about your favorite teacher in high school. If they only taught classes on Saturdays would you still want to be in their class? Some of you may say absolutely no but some of you may think twice before you answer.

I pay a lot of money to go to college and I want the best experience I can get. I scheduled my classes to all start no earlier than 10am. I didn't pay attention to which professor was teaching the class. Bad idea! I ended up with the devil for a professor for one of my classes. It only met two times a week, perfect, and it didn't start until 11am, again perfect. I got to sleep in and take my time each morning before class. However, for the entire semester, **two times a week I paid to meet with the devil**.

When it came time to schedule classes for the next semester I decided to do some research. I went online to a website where professors are rated by former students. I looked through each professor and read the reviews for all of them. I found one that had all A+ ratings. Perfect! I went online to schedule my classes and the professor taught only 1 night a week for three hours and on the biggest party night of the week. Noooooo! What were the chances? I thought to myself, 'what the heck, I'll sign up and if it is really miserable I'll just drop the class.'

The semester began. As all of my friends were getting dressed up and ready to go out I was throwing on some sweatpants and getting my books together to head to class. Maybe this was a bad idea. Well, I went to class and within ten minutes I already knew I made the right choice. The professor was so cool. It was so obvious he loved to teach and even more obvious that he loved what he was teaching. Before I knew it the three hours had gone by. How is that possible? Did I really just enjoy three hours of class while all my friends are out partying? Yes, I did! By the end of the semester I had learned more in that class than I had learned from most of my other classes. I got an A in the class because I enjoyed the work I was doing. I didn't work hard just to get the A. I worked hard because I liked what I was learning and my professor made it interesting. The unfortunate part of this story is that this was during the second semester of my junior year. I only had one more year to schedule for classes. Imagine if I had picked all of my professors the first two years based on their ratings and not just by the time of the class. I would have learned so much more, enjoyed going to class and definitely would have avoided the devil. Before I came to college I wish I had known to base my classes on who taught them, not on what time they were offered.

PROFESSIONAL RELATIONSHIPS WITH PROFESSORS

I wish I had a closer professional relationship with some of my professors or other faculty at my school. Internships and jobs sometimes require recommendations. A friend of mine got a great internship because a professor recommended her to an internship program. If I had proved myself in the classroom and made a point of meeting my professors, maybe would have been more willing to help out when I was applying for internships.

PROFESSORS REALLY DO HELP

I wish I knew that the professors are willing to help students throughout the semester and even after they graduate. I know it may sound strange. Professors are supposed to be helping us throughout college. Unfortunately even I got caught up in thinking that professors were only there to teach in the classroom. Freshman year I would go to class, listen to the professor and when class was over I would leave to go on with the rest of my day. One day I was working on an assignment for a class and was getting so frustrated because I couldn't figure out what to do. I talked to some of my friends in the class to see if they knew what to do. Nobody had an answer. I was so frustrated that I called my Mom in tears. After she calm me down she suggested I e-mail my professor. E-mail my professor? No way! But, I decided I had to. I sent him an e-mail explaining that I was unclear of what the assignment was and I couldn't figure out where to begin. He e-mailed me back by the end of the day and suggested I meet with him in his office to go over the work.

When the time came I got my work together and went to his office. **I couldn't believe how helpful he was.** He explained everything and made the assignment a lot more clear. He complemented me on the fact that I made the effort to reach out to him. He assumed that because I couldn't understand what the assignment was there were probably many more students who were confused as well. In class the next day he explained the assignment again and even gave us an extension for when it was due.

I ended up meeting with him throughout the semester to go over assignments. I even brought my study guide to him to make sure I was studying the right materials. The more I met with him the more I saw what he did for other students. One time when I went to his office I had to wait a few minutes while he was talking with somebody else. I found out it was a former student of his that was asking for advice on a new job he wanted. The professor was helping him with his resume and giving him some names of people he knew that may be able to help him get the job. It made me think about what I would do when I needed a job. It also made me realize that my professors weren't there to just teach us in the classroom. I wish I knew this before college because I would have met with my professors more often. They are truly the best resources.

I wish I knew professors aren't scary. They are normal people just like me.

SOME PROFESSORS DON'T CARE

I wish I knew that not every professor was going to know my name, or care to know my name for that matter. Before college I was every teacher's dream student. In their eyes I seemed to do everything right and was a model student. I loved being close with my teachers and being able to feel connected to them in the classroom. I liked being able to have a huge voice and make an impact. In college, how a student performs is all on them. Professors at my college are more like advisors. I have a lot of large lecture halls and my professors just tell the students how to do something and when to do it. Even into my second year of college I expected my professors to take care of the students. I think I was hoping more than expecting.

There are positives and negatives to this idea of professors really knowing their students. In a way, even though it was a huge culture shock for me, it taught me independence. One thing I will leave college with that I did not have before is the ability to **go out into the work force without anyone guiding me or holding my hand.** My teachers in high school were comforting because they were always there. I guess if all of my professors were like that, I would be far from prepared to take on the world after I graduate.

GET WHAT YOU PAY FOR

I wish I knew how much I would enjoy learning and I wish I took advantage of the amazing opportunities to learn while in college. An education is one of the most valuable things in life. There is something extremely rewarding about learning new information. Freshman year I just went through the motions and complained about classes the way that most college students complained. It wasn't until my junior year that I told myself I really wanted to do well in my classes. I did all of my work, I made study guides, and I began to participate in class more. My classes became more enjoyable, I felt like I was growing intellectually and I ended up doing the best that year than I had done any other semester. Learning is fun. You will be paying thousands and thousands of dollars to get an education. Don't just go through the motions. Get what you are paying for.

EENY, MEENY MINEY, MAJOR

I wish I knew how hard it was going to be to decide a major. I applied as a business student. I originally wanted to work in business because I imagined myself wearing the coolest business suits and walking into a marble foyer of a high rise building. After I took my first business course I ran as fast as I could. I quickly changed my major to communications because I thought being a news person was cool. I quickly learned that getting a job in communications was nearly impossible. I also started to get worried about my loans that were building up and how much money I would have to pay back after college. I realized **that if I didn't love what I was doing and it wasn't my passion, then maybe I should change my major.**

I thought about what I really liked to do. I would love to teach! I would love to be able to coach teams and I couldn't think of anything better than having my summers off. I looked into English and the potential of being a teacher. I really like English but I wasn't sure if what I wanted to teach. I met with the education department to ask how to program worked. They were so welcoming and so organized. They told me how to apply for the education program and that if I got in I would be able to learn the difference about teaching high school and middle school. I applied for the program and got in! I got to try everything in my first few classes and when I had to choose between focusing as a middle school teacher or a high school teacher I knew exactly what I wanted. You can only imagine what my parents were thinking through all of this. They told me that I had to make a decision and stick with it or they would pull me out of college. I wanted to graduate on time. The longer I stayed in college the longer my loans would pile up.

As a college senior, I still am not sure where my life is taking me (don't tell my parents). I keep my head up and my eyes open because I never know what will fall into my lap. There are many options in life and I know that something will eventually work out.

MORE CLASSES, HARDER CLASSES

I wish I knew that classes get harder as you get older. I wish I knew to work as hard as I could my freshman and sophomore year because those were the easiest classes. That would have been an easy way to bring up my GPA early. As you get older you add more to your plate, the biggest piece being the job search. Looking for a job and networking with people takes a lot of time. Classes aren't always first priority as you begin doing job interviews and work on getting your foot in the "real world." By working hard the first couple of years your GPA should be solid. Not getting all A's as a junior and senior won't hurt you overall.

Consider this... every May, every year there are thousands and thousands of college students graduating which means there are thousands and thousands of young adults looking for work. **Having a 4.0 GPA and a diploma isn't enough to get you a job these days.** You need to have more on your resume. So, focus on academics the first couple of years so you can spread your wings a little as you get older and not have to stress about getting your GPA back up.

I wish I knew to get to class early to get the seat that I wanted.

PART V

FOOD

MONEY

CAMPUS

FAT BOY

I wish I knew how easy it is to get out of shape. Days and weeks go by extremely fast and before I knew it, it had been over a month since I'd done any form of exercise. The combination of being lazy and drinking three or four nights a week, sometimes more, took its toll on my body. **It was so easy to get distracted from my personal health** and forget to take care of myself. Most of my friends and I were on a sports team in high school and didn't have to think twice about being active. Now those daily practices and off season workouts don't exist. Even with a gut, it's hard to motivate myself to get active when nobody is telling me I have to.

FRESHMAN FIFTEEN, NO JOKE

I wish I knew that the freshman fifteen is in fact real! I promised myself it wouldn't happen to me, but it did. It's difficult to stay healthy and fit during college. The dining hall has endless options that you cannot pass up. There's ice cream, French fries, pizza, and a full selection of candy. Yes, I could stay active and get to the gym but **who wants to go to the gym when it's cold, raining or snowing**. Trust me it wasn't hard for me to find an excuse to skip the gym. On top of the greasy foods and lack of working out, going out three nights a week doesn't help either. Where there was beer, there was always late night eating. I told myself to watch out for the freshman fifteen but I clearly lost sight of that. If I had stayed active and ate food in moderation I would not be where I am today; 3 pants sizes bigger. Being healthy would have made me feel much better and improve my lifestyle at college. I wish I made the gym my best friend.

NO MORE PASTA

I wish I knew how to cook. Freshman and sophomore year was fine because I had a meal plan. The minute I moved off campus I had to rely on only myself for food. My roommates weren't going to cook me anything; they too could barely cook for themselves. Because I do not know how to cook any fancy meals, I have made and consumed pasta every single day this semester. I am extremely sick of all sorts of pasta and really wish I knew other foods that I can make that don't involve pasta or microwaves.

I GOT FAT

I wish I knew how fat I would get. Freshman year was an exciting time in my life. I came to school, I met new friends, I went to class, I partied all the time, and I went to bed when I wanted to. I drank as much as I wanted, I ate as much as I wanted, and I was running my own life. Of all of those factors the biggest issue was that I was certainly eating as much as I wanted. In high school I ate when I had free time but between school, sports, and work the free time

I had to eat was spread out throughout the day. In college there was more free time than I knew what to do with.

In the beginning of the year when meeting new friends it was easy to socialize when food was around. A group of us would get together and have breakfast together, lunch, snacks and so on. At home I was limited to whatever was in my refrigerator or pantry. **At the school cafeteria there were more options than I could imagine.** For example, for breakfast there was anything from bagels, to muffins, to omelets, bacon, sausage, waffles and everything in between. Of course when this was presented to me I went for the most delicious, buttery, fatty foods. I would swipe my ID card to pay for my meal and then enjoyed every bite of it. Now, in addition to the plethora of food in the cafeteria there was more that was added to my diet.

As a college student I was staying up late, the more hours awake the more time I had to snack on food. When I would go out and party with my friends the night always ended in pizza delivery. After a night of drinking the best way to end the night was with a warm, cheesy pizza. I swear that it helps lessen the hangover for the next day too.

When thanksgiving break rolled around and I went home for the holiday I went to my closet to pack up some winter clothes to bring back to school. I grabbed my favorite pair of jeans, started to put them on and BOOM – I was fat! They didn't fit. I couldn't believe it. I stepped on the scale and in fact I had gained 12 pounds! The "Freshman 15" was no longer a myth. It was my reality. At college with the variety of foods to pick from I picked the unhealthiest, every night after drinking calorie filled beer I was shoving pizza into my stomach and stopping at the candy section in the student center was part of my normal day.

When I went back to school I got my butt into shape. I watched what I ate and I went to the gym as often as I could. The weight started to come off but it wasn't easy. If only I had watched what I was eating when I first came to college. Don't get sucked in by the "freshman 15" or else you'll literally be sucking in to look good. I wish I knew that my college lifestyle would make me fat!

LOVE MY FOOD

I wish I knew that the school I go to is not a buffet style of eating. When I was looking at colleges when I was in high school I always looked at the food that was in the cafeteria. I never thought about how much the food actually cost. The cafeteria at my college is not a free for all. I have to pay for everything that I want. Some days I am starving but if I actually ate what I wanted to at each meal my meal money would be drained way before the semester was over. I didn't really consider how much my eating style would change through school and I wish I had paid more attention to the food and the actual meal plan when I was taking campus tours.

CHEAP FOOD

I wish I knew that the cheapest food is the worst food. I know it is kind of a commonly known fact. All the fast food restaurants are the worst for you no matter where you go but it's easy to forget that when you are standing in the middle of the cafeteria at school. Aside from the fact that the unhealthiest food options are usually the best tasting they are also the cheapest. My meal money runs out fast so I usually pick the cheapest food so that my money lasts me longer. Hamburgers, chicken fingers, french fries, pizza, and grilled cheese are the cheapest. No place on that list is the salad bar or the sandwiches. Yes, I saved some money but I sacrificed a few pant sizes. It is not worth saving a few extra bucks to then go up a few extra pounds.

I wish I knew that cookies, macaroni and cheese, and pizza become a food group.

MONEY NEVER GROWS ON TREES

I wish I knew that money really doesn't grow on trees. Before college I never really had a problem with feeling like I was broke and out of money. When I got to college I had a rude awakening. Without my parents to back me up everything seems more expensive. It was a hard adjustment and I began to have a much **greater appreciation for my parents supporting me.** Yes, college is a lot of fun but that fun is definitely not always free.

I wish I knew that spending money every weekend will bankrupt your account faster than you think.

BUDGETING ON
A DOLLAR

I wish I knew how expensive it was to maintain a life at college. Every little thing costs money and I had no idea how to budget. I knew I wasn't going to have a lot of money so I saved a lot from working over the summer. I didn't realize how poor I would be at college, even with the amount of money I had saved. I thought paying tuition was enough but it really wasn't. There were costs for buying anything else I needed for my dorm room, groceries, books, and for social activities. No, social activities aren't mandatory but watching TV movies in my room every Friday and Saturday night was the last thing I wanted to do. By social activities I don't mean going to clubs and bars every night. It costs money for casual nights also like going out to dinner, going to a movie, or going to the mall to shop. My friends and I do go to clubs but thankfully we don't go out every weekend because that is where we spent the most money.

After a few drinks, money started to have no value to us. It's kind of scary. The first time we went out to a club I spent $100 without even realizing it. It would have been helpful to take a business class in high school to learn more about budgeting. I also should have just sat with my parents to go over budgeting. I never had to worry about money when I was home because I either had my parents to help me pay for stuff or I picked up extra hours at work to make some more money. I began to limit the amount of cash I brought with me when I went out with my friends. I'd also leave my ATM card at home. That way I only used what I brought with me. I was more aware of what I was spending. It really is crazy how hard it is to maintain a life at college when you are making hardly any money.

OOPS

I wish I knew what I actually wanted to do with my life before wasting my parent's money to go to college. As I sit through business classes all day all I can think about is how I really would never like to work in an office. My parents are paying thousands of dollars for me to go to college to get a business degree and I never want to work in business.

LAST MINUTE COLLEGE CHANGE

I wish I knew what kind of school I would like. When deciding on a college I wasn't really sure what I was looking for. I didn't know if I wanted a big school or a small school; a campus or a city. I narrowed my choices based on what my friends had said. That was probably the worst idea ever. I had a great friend who went to a school in a city. She would always say how much she loved it and how she is going to stay in the city even after graduation. I think because she loved it so much, it made me think that I would love it just as much.

I decided to go to a school in a city. I spent the whole summer before freshman year of college regretting my decision. I'm not a city girl. I don't really love the school. The school was just too big and it did not have the college feel I now know I was looking for. I thought it was too late to change my mind so I spent the whole summer dreading my decision. Each night that I packed my stuff for college I would cry. In addition to the fact that I was leaving my family, I was also headed to a college I knew I was going to hate. However, a week before I was schedule to move in, my parents, tired of seeing how miserable I was, called a different school I had been accepted to to see if they would still accept me. It was a smaller school with a campus feel. It had pretty buildings and a lot of green grass. I was shocked to know my parents had called and even more shocked to know that the school would still accept me *and* give me my scholarship.

I wish I had done my research. I wish I hadn't listened to my friends. This was going to be the next four years of my life and I should have known better than to listen to anyone else other than myself. I wish I was aware of what I really wanted. It is so important to take the time when making the decision to choose a college. There is a college for everyone and I am having the time of my life now. I want every student to have the same experience and get the same feelings from their college as I am from mine. I love my school!

THEY ARE NOT OUT TO GET YA'

I wish I knew I didn't have to watch my back as much as people told me. Everyone said cover your drink at a party, never accept a drink from somebody at a bar, never walk in the parking lot at night, never walk to your dorm by yourself, and don't trust anybody. While it is important to consider all of these points the one thing I wish to share is that it isn't as scary as people told me.

Every time people advised me on this stuff I thought, 'geez, college is like a war zone; everyone is going to be out to get me and all the guys are going to take advantage of me.' But really, it's not that bad. I was always aware of my surroundings because, of course, "what if" but I never found myself in those situations. **Scary music doesn't play in the background as you walk late at night to your dorm.** You don't have to fend off guys running at you from out of the bushes. Security is on every campus and they are prepared for everything. Cell phones keep you constantly connected. When I went to parties the guys never walked around dropping roofies into everybody's drinks. Of course I paid attention to my drink and my surroundings. I always pointed out where the exit was in the room, and yes I never accepted a drink from somebody I didn't know. But it was always precautionary.

So yes, while your parents and other adults will tell you to be careful, do listen to them. Don't worry, even though they tell you those things it's not as though you will be faced with them every day and every weekend. I went to college anxious as to what I would encounter. I was on edge every weekend until I realized the environment wasn't as scary as people made me believe. I was able to relax and enjoy my time. I did get a mini mace key chain. Just in case!

IN FROM THE COLD

I wish I knew how bad the winters really were going to be. No one ever talks about the weather when they are choosing a college but I wish I had. I grew up in Massachusetts and I am used to long winters but I wish I had chosen somewhere a bit warmer than New England when I had the chance. The winters are beautiful and cozy, when you're sitting inside by the fire. It's a lot colder walking to class than you think it will be. When the wind is blowing in your face and you're walking through puddles of partially melted snow with bits of mud mixed in them you will regret going to school in the northeast the way I do. Shoveling your own snow? Not fun! Make sure you double think about how much you can tolerate the ice cold winter. Maybe you're more of a beach bum.

I wish I knew to use some common sense when it came to safety.

CLOSING

College is so much more than the challenges of classes, professors, roommates, studying, and socialization. It includes the good, the bad, the hurt, the love, and every experience in-between. It is a wonderful part of life. You will see yourself mature, evolve and adjust as you realize and identify your true inner core personal values. What makes me most happy is the fact I learned something new each day. I learned academic lessons, personal lessons, as well as what life has to offer, life beyond college.

To make the most of your college experience get to know who you are, what you like, what makes you tick and most of all how to deal with what you imagine. Take risks, try new things and be open to change.

The most important point to learn from this book is that no matter what you are expecting or how much you prepare for your college experience, **always be prepared for a curve ball.**

ABOUT THE AUTHOR

Gabbriel Simone

Gabbriel Simone is the creator of I Wish I Knew It™. She received her Bachelor of Science degree in Accounting from Quinnipiac University in 2010. Gabbriel refused an opportunity offered to work in a large public accounting firm opting to use her business background, passion for learning and love of storytelling to pursue her dream of creating I Wish I Knew It™.

Gabbriel currently works as a college admissions counselor while pursuing a Master of Science degree in Organizational Leadership at Quinnipiac University. Gabbriel's interest in and creative process for *I Wish I Knew It Before Going To College* began while she was an undergraduate. Her motivation to complete the book skyrocketed once she began working in the admissions office. There she quickly learned of the unrealistic expectations that high school students and their parents had concerning the college experience. *I Wish I Knew It Before Going To College* is meant to offer more realistic expectations, give students opportunities to share their experiences and, of course, entertain the reader.

The three pieces of advice that Gabbriel shares are; a) nothing in life will be handed to you, b) you can achieve anything as long as you work for it, and c) stop thinking about it, just do it. Those things most important to her are family, health, happiness, hard work and of course a bit of relaxation. She believes she has found her passion and wants to help others find theirs. "If I can make people more aware of what they are doing each step of their life, I may help them find and understand what makes them happy. If I can help someone identify and appreciate what will keep them happy then support their focus to productively act on that, I feel like I will make a difference. Not everyone gets to wake up and say they love what they do. That doesn't make sense to me. Figure out what you love and do it. That's what life's about."

Gabbriel was born and raised on Long Island, NY and moved to Branford, CT in 2008 where she currently resides. Her parents live in Florida and her older brother, John, who she considers her best friend, lives and teaches in Connecticut.

Be a part of

I Wish I Knew It™

Visit www.iwishiknewit.com
and submit your experience.

We are currently collecting submissions
for and creating the following books:

COLLEGE
I Wish I Knew It
Before Becoming A College Athlete
Before Sending My Child To College
Before Going To Medical School
Before Going to Law School

While we are not yet in the process of
creating the following books we *are*
collecting submissions for these future titles:

LIFE
I Wish I Knew It
Before Getting Married
Before Becoming a Mom
Before Becoming a Dad
Before Dating Long Distance

CAREER
I Wish I Knew It
Before Working For Corporate America
Before Working in a Hospital
Before Becoming a Teacher

Check on our website for future titles, sample stories and any updates about I Wish I Knew It™.

www.iwishiknewit.com

BUY A SHARE OF THE FUTURE IN YOUR COMMUNITY

These certificates make great holiday, graduation and birthday gifts that can be personalized with the recipient's name. The cost of one S.H.A.R.E. or one square foot is $54.17. The personalized certificate is suitable for framing and will state the number of shares purchased and the amount of each share, as well as the recipient's name. The home that you participate in "building" will last for many years and will continue to grow in value.

Here is a sample SHARE certificate:

YES, I WOULD LIKE TO HELP!

*I support the work that Habitat for Humanity does and I want to be part of the excitement! As a donor, I will receive periodic updates on your construction activities but, more importantly, I know my gift will help a family in our community realize the dream of homeownership. **I would like to SHARE in your efforts against substandard housing in my community!** (Please print below)*

PLEASE SEND ME _____ SHARES at $54.17 EACH = $ $_____

In Honor Of: _____

Occasion: (Circle One)   HOLIDAY   BIRTHDAY   ANNIVERSARY

   OTHER: _____

Address of Recipient: _____

Gift From: _____ *Donor Address:* _____

Donor Email: _____

I AM ENCLOSING A CHECK FOR $ $_____ PAYABLE TO HABITAT FOR HUMANITY **OR** PLEASE CHARGE MY VISA OR MASTERCARD *(CIRCLE ONE)*

Card Number _____ Expiration Date: _____

Name as it appears on Credit Card _____ Charge Amount $ _____

Signature _____

Billing Address _____

Telephone # Day _____ Eve _____

PLEASE NOTE: Your contribution is tax-deductible to the fullest extent allowed by law.
Habitat for Humanity • P.O. Box 1443 • Newport News, VA 23601 • 757-596-5553
www.HelpHabitatforHumanity.org

CPSIA information can be obtained at www.ICGtesting.com
Printed in the USA
BVOW020302130112

280307BV00001B/3/P